POLITICOS

———

A Play in One Act

by

Paolo Mazzucato

Playwright Edition

Performance

This Playwright Edition may be used in its entirety for student, amateur or non-profit theatrical productions, without royalty fee.

Notification of place (city, state, theater) and date of performance must, however, be sent to info@bepibooks.com. Acknowledgement of playwright should be included on program or promotional notices.

Equity or For-Profit productions may inquire about any applicable royalty fees at info@bepibooks.com

All other rights, outside of the above prescribed performance rights, are reserved, including the rights to reproduce this book or portions thereof in any form whatsoever, including but not limited to print, audio, and electronic. For more information contact info@bepibooks.com

© 1987 by Paolo Mazzucato

Production Note

POLITICOS by Paolo Mazzucato premiered in 1988 in the New Works and New Genres Series at the Organic Theater in Chicago, Illinois.

ISBN-13: 978-1-7336406-3-3

Cast of Characters

<u>Weber</u>: an uncertain man in an uncertain time

<u>Ash</u>: Weber's friend

<u>Una</u>: a woman who asks questions

<u>Voice</u>: a disembodied voice/an unseen watcher

<u>Beggar</u>: a poor man, in need of legs

<u>Rich Man</u>: a rich man, in need of a favor

Setting

A desert landscape

SCENE 1

(The lights fade up to suggest mid-day. WEBER sits center stage on a rock. He is dressed plainly. He is looking at a tattered map which he turns side to side trying to pinpoint his location on it. After a minute or so, a disembodied VOICE breaks the silence as it filters into the theatre through a speaker.)

VOICE
Hi, how are you?

WEBER
(Hesitantly.) I'm fine… How are you?

VOICE
Just fine thanks. I was just wondering… do you know what time it is?

WEBER
No, I'm sorry, my watch stopped working about two weeks ago.

VOICE
No, I mean year time… What year is it?

WEBER
Oh…uh…no, I'm sorry, we lost track of that years ago. Actually my father's father used to follow that sort of thing but no one bothers anymore.

VOICE

I see. Well I suppose it doesn't really matter. (Long pause.)

    (WEBER stares strangely out over the audience, looking for the source of the VOICE.)

WEBER

Why?

VOICE

Why what?

WEBER

Why doesn't it matter?

VOICE

Well time is a relative dimension. The course of human existence, human motivation and human activity remains an unchangeable cycle uninfluenced by the abstract passage and subtle didactic messages presented through time.

WEBER

(Long pause.) Oh. (Squinting.) Where are you?

VOICE

I'm up in the booth. (Pause.) Where are you?

WEBER

You can't see me either?

VOICE

It looks like a desert down there, symbolically representative of the stagnant condition of human existence with no attempt to make fertile ground for future generations.

WEBER

(Looking around.) Does it? I suppose you're right. What's your name?

VOICE

What's yours?

WEBER

I asked first.

VOICE

And first is always the toughest.

WEBER

What?

VOICE

Being the first, taking initiative, working for a change.

WEBER

Change what?

VOICE

Whatever can be made better. (Pause.) What is your name?

WEBER

Weber.

VOICE
How old are you?

WEBER
Twenty-nine.

VOICE
Who is your father?

WEBER
A great man.

VOICE
What did he do?

WEBER
He opened the cans. (Pause.)

VOICE
What do you do?

WEBER
What?

VOICE
Do. How do you live?

WEBER
How do you mean? I breathe, I live. I'm sorry, I have to go.

(WEBER rises.)

VOICE
And that's life?

WEBER
What...

                    VOICE
Breathing?

                    WEBER
You don't think so? (Pause.) I breathe, I
live.

                    VOICE
And what else?

                    WEBER
What else what?

                    VOICE
Are you happy?

                    WEBER
Happy with what?

                    VOICE
With what's around you.

                    WEBER
(He looks around.) I don't understand.

                    VOICE
Do you ever feel like you should try to make
the world around you a little nicer than
what it is, for others as well as for
yourself?

                    WEBER
I can't do that.

                    VOICE
Why not?

                    WEBER
Because…I don't.

                    VOICE
I see. Are you alone?

                    WEBER
(He looks around.) I think so.

                    VOICE
Always?

                    WEBER
Oh, I see. No Ash is coming.

                    VOICE
Ash?

                    WEBER
He's a friend. He and me, I mean, I, read (past tense) from the same book. We could catch cockroaches bare-handed, too.

                    VOICE
What does he do?

                    WEBER
Do? What do…I'm sorry, I have to go.

                    VOICE
Who's the person who can change things for you?

                    WEBER
What?

                    VOICE
Is there someone?

                    WEBER
William is on the council for…uh…civil…
improvement.

                    VOICE
William?

                    WEBER
He's a friend. We read (past tense) from the
same book. He and me used to—

                    VOICE
Where is he now?

                    WEBER
He's…uh…left. He's on the council for…uh… He
does important work. He has the power to
make things better for everyone.

                    VOICE
And you?

                    WEBER
I'm sorry, I have to go.

                    VOICE
Where?

                    WEBER
Nowhere.

(ASH enters upstage left.
He is dressed plainly,
like WEBER. He wheels
before him an old bicycle,
which is missing it's back
wheel. He leans it against
the rocks and sits down to
wipe his forehead.)

ASH

Damn hot.

WEBER

What?

ASH

Damn hot.

WEBER

Did you hear him?

ASH

I said, damn hot.

WEBER

Not you, the voice.

ASH

Who?

WEBER

(Over the audience) Hey are you there?

ASH

Damn hot.

(WEBER gives up on the
VOICE and returns to his
spot center stage.)

WEBER

Want an ice cube?

ASH

You have one?

WEBER

(Checks his pockets.) No. (Pause.)

ASH

Wish there was some shade. (Pause.)

WEBER

How?

ASH

A tree would be nice.

WEBER

A tree?

ASH

Yes. A big oak tree with big, black branches and leaves, leaves on the branches. (Pause.) We could call it George.

WEBER

(Sits on his rock.) Where's your hat? (Pause.)

ASH

Do you have any more soup?

                    WEBER
Two cans. (Reflectively.) What do you do?

                    ASH
What?

                    WEBER
What do you...I was talking to someone and he—

                    ASH
Who?

                    WEBER
Are you breathing?

                    ASH
(Breathes on his hand.) Yes.

                    WEBER
Why do you suppose that is? (Pause.)

                    ASH
Where's your hat?

                    WEBER
Do you suppose we should be doing something?

                    ASH
Like what?

                    WEBER
Like (Long pause.) I don't know... I just
think we should.

                    ASH
You don't make sense.

                        WEBER
Suppose you're not happy.

                        ASH
Who says?

                        WEBER
Just suppose. How would you go about it?

                        ASH
About what?

                        WEBER
Becoming happy.

                        ASH
No reason to be unhappy.

                        WEBER
But what if you were?

                        ASH
Time goes by, things get better, and then I would be happy.

                        WEBER
And if they didn't get better?

                        ASH
They would.

                        WEBER
Just suppose.

                        ASH
Then William should do something.

                    WEBER
(Excitedly.) Exactly! That's what I thought.

                     ASH
Now you don't?

                    WEBER
I don't know. They said not to… We need more
soup I think.

                     ASH
Soup.

                    WEBER
You think William could do something?

                     ASH
Of course.

                    WEBER
How do you know? (Pause.)

                     ASH
He was trained to know how. (Pause.) Are you
unhappy?

                    WEBER
Perhaps we should go talk to William.

                     ASH
Perhaps. (Pause.) Should we go soon?

                    WEBER
Yes… (Pause.) We should go now.

(ASH nods. WEBER waits. Neither moves. WEBER considers. Then, they both turn and begin to move off in opposite directions— WEBER, stage right; ASH, stage left. They stop. They turn and look at each other.)

(Lights fade out.)

Scene 2

(Later that day. The lights fade up on a setting very similar to the one before. WEBER and ASH enter from stage left. ASH is wheeling his bicycle before him.)

WEBER

It's broken.

ASH

What?

WEBER

It's broken.

ASH

How?

                    WEBER
Where's the back wheel?

                    ASH
If I find one, I'll put it on.

                    WEBER
And if you don't?

                    ASH
Can we rest a bit?

                    WEBER
Just suppose—

                    ASH
Just a bit won't hurt.

                         (WEBER sighs and sits on
                         the ground, facing off
                         stage left. ASH sets his
                         bicycle down.)

                    ASH
Do you have an ice cube?

                         (UNA enters stage right
                         with a picnic basket. She
                         is a woman in her
                         twenties. She is dressed
                         simply but neatly. She
                         sits downstage right.)

                    WEBER
Why don't you just—

                    ASH
Who's that?

WEBER
Hmm?

ASH
Shhhh… she might—

WEBER
(Turns.) Who?

ASH
She has a basket.

UNA
Hello. (Silence.)

WEBER
Hi.

ASH
Hello.

WEBER
Hello.

(UNA sits and opens her picnic basket. ASH inches closer. WEBER rises.

WEBER
You wouldn't happen to have a can of soup, would you?

ASH
Or two?

UNA
Would you like to join me?

(She pulls out a loaf of
bread from her basket.
WEBER sits near her. ASH
watches curiously.)

WEBER
This is very nice of you. What is your name?

UNA
What's yours?

WEBER
I asked…Weber.

(She gives him a piece
from the loaf. ASH sits
quickly.)

ASH
Ash. My name is Ash.

(She gives him some bread.
He eats hungrily.)

UNA
Where are you both going?

WEBER
We're going to talk to William on the
council of…He can make things better.

UNA
Really? Better for who?

WEBER
For me, for you…for everyone, I suppose.

                    UNA
Couldn't you?

                    WEBER
What?

                    UNA
Couldn't you make things better yourself?

                    WEBER
Myself?

                    UNA
...Or together with Ash.

                    WEBER
Ash?

                    ASH
(Pauses from eating.) What?

                    WEBER
I suppose...No, I can't.

                    ASH
(Shaking his head.) He can't. (He continues to eat.)

                    UNA
Why's that?

                    WEBER
Because...well, that's what William does. He makes things better.

                    UNA
Really? How can he do that?

WEBER
Well he...uh... (He looks at ASH for assistance.)

ASH
(Pauses from eating.) He was trained for that sort of thing.

UNA
Really? How was he trained? (Pause.)

WEBER
He...they chose him to do it.

UNA
They didn't choose you?

WEBER
No I can't...You see, William can change things.

ASH
Do you have a salty sardine by any chance? (He looks in the basket.)

UNA
But can't you change things?

WEBER
I'm not on the council.

UNA
And so?

WEBER
And so, I can't change things.

UNA
You're sure?

WEBER
You're not? (He looks at ASH for assistance.)

ASH
(Looking up briefly from the picnic basket.) You're not?

WEBER
(To UNA.) I am. I think.

UNA
I see. (pause.)

>   (UNA takes the loaf of
>   bread from the basket
>   again and breaks it in
>   two. She lays the two
>   pieces on the ground
>   before WEBER and ASH.)

UNA (CONT)
I could change things for you.

WEBER
You?

>   (ASH takes the piece of
>   bread uncertainly.)

WEBER
You're on the council?

UNA
No.

WEBER
Well then how could you possibly—

(ASH eats. WEBER considers.)

UNA
Do I need to be on the council?

WEBER
Yes, of course. That's how…it is.

UNA
Suppose it's not.

WEBER
What do you…I don't see.

UNA
I know.

WEBER
Know what? (Pause.)

UNA
Why can't you and Ash, do for each other, what the council hasn't done.

WEBER
Hasn't? (Defensively.) But…they have, they do, I think…I know.

UNA
(She sighs.) Then I must show you.

                        (ASH returns to the picnic
                        basket.)

                        WEBER
What?

                        UNA
(Pause.) Are you unhappy?

                        WEBER
How?

                        UNA
What should change?

                        WEBER
Change? Oh, I don't… things. Soup, for
example. Everyone should have enough soup.

                        ASH
(Pulling a can from the basket excitedly.)
Clam chowder!

                        UNA
That's a very good thing. Why aren't you on
the council?

                        WEBER
No, William is on the council.

                        UNA
What has he done?

                        WEBER
(Defensively.) What has… He does good
things. He told me so. He helps people, he
protects people… uh… he wants truth and
justice, he wants to keep people happy.

                    UNA
Are you happy?

                    ASH
Excuse me, but if you don't mind, I'd really
like to have this clam chowder. It's been so
long since I've had anything like it. I
remember—

                    WEBER
I'm sorry, we have to go. Ash give back the
food.

                    UNA
How do you live?

                    ASH
Clam chowder.

                    WEBER
What?

                    UNA
Do. What do you do?

                    WEBER
Why do you ask that sort of—

                    ASH
So, how 'bout it?

                    UNA
(Referring to the can.) It's yours.

(ASH digs through the basket looking for a can opener. WEBER stands and crosses downstage left to look out over the audience, squinting as if searching for the VOICE again. He turns back towards UNA.)

WEBER
Where…? What is your name?

UNA
Didn't I say?

WEBER
Did you? No, I don't think so.

ASH
Excuse me, you wouldn't happen to have a can opener?

(UNA reaches into the basket without looking and takes out a can opener. She hands it to ASH. He opens the can and eats, oblivious to the conversation around him.)

UNA
(To WEBER.) If you were on the council what would *you* do?

WEBER
William is on the council.

                    UNA
Just suppose.

                    WEBER
I can't. I would have to be chosen to… (He
turns out toward the audience.) I could give
everyone soup.

                    UNA
Everyone?

                    WEBER
(He turns to UNA.) Well, everyone who needed
some.

                    UNA
Where would it all come from?

                    WEBER
What? From…people.

                    UNA
Suppose no one wanted to give you any soup.

                    WEBER
They would have to.

                    UNA
And if they couldn't?

                    WEBER
Why ask me? William takes care of things
like that.

                    UNA
I see. Does William give you soup?

(ASH offers WEBER some
soup.)

ASH

Have some clam chowder.

(WEBER turns away slowly
and looks out over the
audience again. ASH
continues to eat.)

WEBER

What if I was on the…

UNA

…council.

(Lights fade out.)

Scene 3

(Later the same day. The
lights fade up on a scene
similar to the one before.
ASH kneels downstage
right, next to his bicycle
—turned upside down so
that he can examine the
loose crank. UNA enters
and crosses down to him.)

UNA

Is it broken?

ASH
Broken?

UNA
Does it work?

ASH
It doesn't have a back wheel.

UNA
And so it doesn't work?

ASH
Do you have more soup? (Pause.)

UNA
Can you fix it?

ASH
No, William will know.

UNA
He will fix your bike too?

ASH
Of course.

UNA
Are you sure?

ASH
Am I sure?

UNA
Sure.

ASH
I am. I think.

                    UNA
I see.

                    ASH
(Pause.) William can do everything.

                    UNA
He must be quite powerful.

                    ASH
That's why they chose him.

                    UNA
Really? What if it was the other way around?

                    ASH
What?

                    UNA
Powerful because he was chosen.

                    ASH
(Considers.) And not chosen because he was powerful?

                    UNA
Exactly.

                    ASH
I don't know.

                    UNA
Suppose that it was *that* way.

                    ASH
Well, then anyone could be chosen.

UNA
Even you?

ASH
No, not me.

UNA
Why not you?

ASH
I wasn't trained.

UNA
How was William trained?

ASH
He… well, they liked him, he was chosen.

UNA
I see.

ASH
I suppose I could be chosen. After all, I read (past tense) from the same book.

UNA
Then what would you do?

ASH
I don't know.

UNA
Your bike?

ASH
Exactly. I would have William fix my bike.

UNA

No, a new bike.

ASH

Exactly. I would get a new bike with a back wheel. Everyone would get a bicycle.

UNA

All the same? Remember you're the one they chose.

ASH

Of course. I would get the best one, but only because I work harder.

UNA

Of course.

ASH

You think I would get chosen?

UNA

Do you want some soup?

(ASH stares out over the audience and doesn't answer. WEBER enters from stage left carrying a small cardboard box. He stops at center stage, smiling uncomfortably, ear to ear.)

WEBER

Hello, hello my friends. I thought I might find you here basking in the sun of our fair countryside.

ASH
Where's your hat?

(WEBER takes a can of soup from his box and offers it to ASH.)

WEBER
Would you like some soup my friend? Beef and potato?

(ASH crosses to WEBER at center and takes the can.)

ASH
You don't look good. What happened?

WEBER
I'm fine, how are you? I hope you are enjoying the day.

UNA
Weber, this is Ash.

(WEBER's smile suddenly relaxes as if he is suddenly released from a trance.)

WEBER
Ash? (Pause.) Oh yes of course. I'm sorry. I didn't see you.

ASH
Didn't see me?

					WEBER
Well, I mean…see, I've been busy. I've got
my whole strate…strage…plan worked out. If
people get what they want, they will want to
choose me.

					ASH
Choose you for what?

					WEBER
Council. Just like William, but I'll be—

					ASH
Council! No! You can't be on the—

					WEBER
Council—

					ASH
No, you can't.

					WEBER
What?

					ASH
I don't want you to do it. I have to.

					WEBER
You? No, no, the council is for me.

					ASH
Why?

					WEBER
Because…I know how to do.

					ASH
Do what?

(UNA look out over the
audience from her position
downstage right.)

UNA
Their eyes are closed.

(WEBER and ASH turn toward
UNA.)

WEBER & ASH
(Simultaneously.) Closed?

UNA
I can't wake them.

WEBER
We aren't sleeping.

UNA
But their eyes are closed.

ASH
Where's your hat?

UNA
Human existence, motivation, activity…

WEBER
Wait, what are you—

UNA
…an unchangeable cycle.

ASH
Cycle? Yes, a new bike for everyone!

UNA
The end will make you see.

WEBER
Stop! You don't make sense. No one makes sense. I'll be on the council and make sense.

ASH
And make soup?

(WEBER looks sharply at ASH, grabs his can of soup, and crosses to stage left.)

ASH
(Flustered.) Fine, I don't like potatoes anyways.

WEBER
Well, you'll never get soup from my council.

ASH
They give me hives.

WEBER
Bye Ash.

ASH
Goodbye Weber.

(Lights fade out.)

Scene 4

(Later that day. The lights fade up on a scene similar to the one before. A disheveled BEGGAR is huddled downstage left. He holds a tin mug in his hand. He wears dark sunglasses. He has no legs. WEBER and UNA enter stage right.)

WEBER
And so a soup shortage or a strike by the United Soupers would result in a decrease in availability of soup so I would have no choice but to cut back on distribution for a while.

UNA
I see.

WEBER
But that would never happen.

UNA
Just suppose.

BEGGAR
(Wailing.) Who's there?

(WEBER notices the BEGGAR.)

BEGGAR
I said, who's there?

(The BEGGAR looks around, seemingly blind. Finding no response, he gives up. He sits motionless, looking forward.)

WEBER
(To UNA.) What do you suppose he wants?

UNA
Why don't you ask him?

WEBER
I don't know who he is.

UNA
He's a poor, blind beggar with no legs.

WEBER
Do you know him?

UNA
Everyone does, though some won't admit it.

WEBER
Why?

BEGGAR
(Looking out over the audience.) Hello?

WEBER
(To UNA.) Do you think he might choose me for council?

UNA
(She sighs.) He is one of many.

WEBER
Then I should talk to him.

UNA
I suppose you will.

(UNA exits stage right.
WEBER approaches the
BEGGAR.)

WEBER
Who are you?

BEGGAR
Who are you?

(WEBER turns toward the
audience and the wide,
trance-like smile returns
to his face.)

WEBER
I am Weber, good sir. I am struggling to
help the whole of humanity by aiding all
people in their pursuit of happiness in this
fine land we live in.

BEGGAR
(Looking around.) You call this fine land?
It looks like a desert to me.

(WEBER's smile vanishes.)

WEBER
Does it? (Looks around.) I suppose. You can
see?

                    BEGGAR
See what?

                    WEBER
See, see. You're not blind?

                    BEGGAR
(Sarcastically.) Do I look blind?

                    WEBER
Well…

                    BEGGAR
(As if quoting.) Blindness is in the eyes of the beholder.

                    WEBER
What?

                    BEGGAR
You like? That's a quote from someone famous or something.

                    WEBER
Oh.

                    BEGGAR
That'll be one egg and a slice of white bread.

                    WEBER
What?

                    BEGGAR
An egg and a slice of white bread. You don't think I give out my knowledge for nothing do you?

WEBER
The quote?

BEGGAR
Plus the explanation, that was extra.

WEBER
Oh. Well, how about if I gave you a nice can of soup?

BEGGAR
What kind?

WEBER
Beef and potato.

(The BEGGAR takes the can.)

BEGGAR
What else?

WEBER
What else what?

BEGGAR
What else will you give me?

WEBER
If you choose me to be on the council for… uh…the council—

BEGGAR
Council! They came before—a while back. They were no help at all. Said I needed to learn to stand on my own two feet.

(They pause. The BEGGAR
and WEBER look down at the
beggar's missing legs.)

BEGGAR (CONT)

You ask if *I'm* blind? William, I think his
name was. He walked right past me. He said I
didn't exist. And I just asked for an egg
that time.

WEBER

(Excitedly.) You met William?

BEGGAR

(Angrily.) Damn lousy bit of a person.

(WEBER pauses
uncomfortably. His
campaign smile returns.)

WEBER

Oh, most definitely. I've dealt with him
before. That's why you need to choose me.
I'm working for the good of all people
whether they exist or not. I am struggling
to aid the pursuit of happiness in this
fine…desert.

BEGGAR

What can you do for me?

WEBER

I'm working for the whole of humanity.

BEGGAR

Wonderful, and for me?

WEBER
Well, what would you like?

BEGGAR
I would like my legs back.

WEBER
Your legs? I...can't... (Pause.) I can't see why you haven't gotten them by now. That would be the first thing I did if I were on the council.

BEGGAR
Really? Well I'd appreciate it then.

WEBER
No problem. You've obviously been neglected by the council and it's time for a change.

(WEBER begins to cross away to exit stage right.)

BEGGAR
Hail, hail.

WEBER
Soon, with my official help, you will be standing on your own two feet.

(WEBER exits stage right.)

BEGGAR
Hail, hail. (Pause.) (Calling after WEBER.) You wouldn't happen to have a can opener, would you?

(The BEGGAR tries to open the can on the ground with no success.)

(Lights fade out.)

Scene 5

(Later that day. The lights fade up in a way to suggest late afternoon. WEBER sits on a rock center stage with his map opened up before him. He studies it intently. He sets it down momentarily to dust off his jacket. He stands and attempts to tidy up his appearance. Suddenly, the VOICE filters into the theatre through the speaker once again.)

VOICE
What are you doing?

(WEBER jumps.)

WEBER
Who?

VOICE
Hello Weber.

WEBER
Oh, it's you.

VOICE
What time is it?

WEBER
Late afternoon I suppose.

VOICE
What are you doing?

WEBER
I was just…straightening up. Where did you go?

VOICE
I'm still here.

WEBER
No, I mean before.

VOICE
Before what?

WEBER
Before…before now.

VOICE
Where were you?

WEBER
When?

VOICE
(Pause.) Before.

WEBER
I've been here all the time.

VOICE
You've gone nowhere, done nothing, since we talked last?

WEBER
Oh, well… we were going to go talk to William first… before. You remember William?

VOICE
Of course.

WEBER
Well, I decided that I should be on the council myself so I could give everyone soup.

VOICE
I see.

WEBER
I'm going to change things so everyone will have enough of what they want.

VOICE
That's a noble motivation.

WEBER
Noble?

VOICE
And you?

WEBER
Me what?

VOICE
What do you want?

WEBER
I want to be on the council. (Pause.)

(WEBER holds out his map.)

WEBER (CONT)
See, my strag…plan is to talk to all the people and find out what they want. Then they'll pick me.

VOICE
I see.

WEBER
When I'm on the council, I'll be able to make it better.

VOICE
Make what better?

WEBER
Everything I change.

VOICE
Do they all want the same thing?

WEBER
What?

VOICE
The people. If some want rain and some want sun, what do you give them?

WEBER
(Pause.) I don't see.

VOICE
Change doesn't always work on the grand scale you idealize.

WEBER
I can't make it rain. I just want some soup.

VOICE
But what if they want rain?

WEBER
Who says they do?

VOICE
Just suppose.

WEBER
Well maybe the people who want sun don't really need sun after all, and only think they do. Then it could rain.

VOICE
But they did want sun. You promised sun.

WEBER
Who says?

VOICE
Will you compromise your position?

WEBER
I don't… what? (Defiantly.) If I say it will rain, then I'll make it rain, and if you don't have a hat, you'll just get wet for a while until we've had enough.

VOICE
How long is a while?

                    WEBER
I'm sorry, I have to go now.

                    (WEBER moves toward stage
                    right.)

                    VOICE
Are you upset?

                    (WEBER stops.)

                    WEBER
What?

                    VOICE
What is your name?

                    WEBER
Weber.

                    VOICE
How old are you?

                    WEBER
Twenty-nine.

                    VOICE
What do you do?

                    (WEBER looks out over the
                    audience, confused. He
                    hesitates, dusts off his
                    jacket, and leaves stage
                    right.)

                    (Lights fade out.)

Scene 6

(Later that day. The lights fade up to suggest late afternoon. The BEGGAR is sitting downstage right. He scoops up sand with his tin cup and pours it out again, watching motionless as the grains pass through his fingers. ASH enters stage left and sees the BEGGAR. He observes him curiously for a moment then crosses to him. UNA enters stage right and crosses to downstage left. She sits symmetrically opposite the BEGGAR and duplicates his movements exactly.)

ASH
(To the BEGGAR.) What are you doing?

UNA
Observing life.

ASH
(Still to the BEGGAR.) What?

UNA
Watching, while everything around me moves with time. Watching, while I remain planted to my place of safety. Watching, unable, or perhaps only unwilling to do what someone must do, but no one does.

ASH

What do you mean? (Pause. No answer.) Are you deaf?

UNA

And blind, and mute, and limbless, though I know what must be done.

>   (ASH takes hold of the BEGGAR's arm and shakes him. The BEGGAR spills all the sand in his lap.)

BEGGAR

Now look what you did.

ASH

Oh, I'm sorry, I thought you were dumb.

BEGGAR

Is that so? Well the brain's not in the feet, you know.

ASH

What?

BEGGAR

I won't charge you for that one. I made it up just now. These things have to simmer a while… get out there and breathe before you can say what they're worth.

>   (UNA rises and crosses to the two.)

ASH

My name is Ash. What's yours?

                    BEGGAR
I have no name. I am one of many, many like
yourself.

                      ASH
Can I call you George?

                      UNA
Hello Ash.

                ASH & BEGGAR
(Simultaneously.) Hello.

                      UNA
Would you like to sit for some soup?

                      ASH
Thank you, but no. A councilor cannot think
of himself. He must strive for the good of
all people.

                    BEGGAR
Whether they exist or not.

                      ASH
(Nodding.) Whether they exist or not.

                    BEGGAR
Hey, are you William?

                      ASH
William...you know him?

                    BEGGAR
Damn lousy bit of a person.

                      ASH
Why do you say that?

                    BEGGAR
He passed me over.

                    ASH
Passed you over? Well… maybe he didn't see
you down there.

                    BEGGAR
Exactly.

                    ASH
But if he didn't see you, it's not his
fault.

                    BEGGAR
Unless he refused to look.

                    UNA
(As if campaigning.) But Ash would not
refuse. He is one of you; he is one with
you. He struggles for all people, the many
like yourself. He is your voice. He would
bring you safety, prosperity and happiness.

                    ASH
(Excitedly.) And if you choose me, everyone
will get a brand new bicycle.

                         (Long pause. UNA and the
                         BEGGAR look strangely at
                         ASH.)

                    BEGGAR
What would I do with a bike? I have no legs.

                    ASH
Well… other people do.

(Long pause. The BEGGAR scoops up a cup of sand and begins to pour it through his fingers again.)

ASH
Are you sure you couldn't use a bicycle?

BEGGAR
Only if Weber was on the council.

ASH
Weber?

BEGGAR
Weber. He said he would get me some new legs if he got chosen.

ASH
New legs? (To UNA.) How can he do that?

UNA
Ambition often fosters preposterous biddings.

ASH
(Long pause.) New legs? Is that what you want?

BEGGAR
And a pair of new shoes to match.

ASH
Good then. If you choose me, I will bring you better legs, legs that will never tire. For as long as you walk they will never be tired.

                    BEGGAR
And a pair of shoes to match?

          (ASH looks at UNA.)

                    ASH
And a pair of shoes to match.

          (Lights fade out.)

          Scene 7

          (Before the lights fade
          up, the grating of metal
          spoons on the insides of
          cans can be heard. The
          lights fade up to suggest
          an early, moonlit evening
          and reveal WEBER sitting
          downstage right and ASH
          sitting downstage left,
          isolated and unaware of
          each other's presence.
          They are finishing a meal—
          a can of soup each, some
          bread. UNA enters from
          upstage left and crosses
          to center. She stands
          quietly; She stands
          unnoticed. She reaches out
          to WEBER and ASH, but they
          shift their backs toward
          her and finish their meal.
          Then they lie down and

(sleep. UNA bows her head disappointedly. She sits wearily and speaks, though no one is there to listen.)

                    UNA
Has it gone too far? It is late… too late for my doubts. Doubts in myself more than in you. Everyone sleeps; everyone wakes, nothing's to worry. (Pause.) Only I am afraid, and weak, and unsure. I am Una… Weber, Ash. Don't forget me, because this… strategem, this plan, has only one end.

                    (UNA rises slowly. She
                    takes a hesitant step
                    toward WEBER, then
                    restrains herself. She
                    crosses and exits stage
                    left. After a brief pause,
                    Weber rises to a sitting
                    position. He takes out his
                    map from a pocket and
                    unfolds it once. He then
                    closes it again with a
                    sigh and sets it aside.
                    ASH also wakes. He stands.
                    He begins to cross toward
                    stage right then sees
                    WEBER. He stops.)

                    ASH
Who's there?

                    WEBER
Who's there?

ASH
Weber?

WEBER
Ash?

(Long pause.)

ASH
What are you doing?

WEBER
Doing?

ASH
It's dark.

WEBER
(Sarcastically.) Is it?

ASH
How was your day?

WEBER
Why?

ASH
Why what?

WEBER
Where have you been?

ASH
Why?

WEBER
Did you go all the way to the hill?

ASH

Maybe. Suppose I did. (Pause.) Did you?

WEBER

Maybe, maybe not.

ASH

Suppose you did. What did you do?

WEBER

You think I'd tell you?

ASH

Why not? (Long pause.) Weber?

WEBER

What?

ASH

Do you suppose William is a good councilor?

WEBER

He said he was.

ASH

Did he?

WEBER

Yes.

ASH

Oh. (Pause.) Why do you suppose he hasn't done anything for anyone?

WEBER

Are you sure?

ASH

What? Well, yes.

WEBER

He just forgot I'm sure. He's very busy.

ASH

(Pause.) Do you suppose… What if the council just doesn't work. Maybe we need to do things ourselves—

(WEBER rises and crosses to ASH.)

WEBER

That's… How can you… Ourselves? We can't make changes ourselves. The council is supposed to do that. They always did. That's what they do—for as long as I can remember. They make things better.

ASH

Are you sure?

WEBER

Yes I'm… Look, see this land? This land is here, you know why? Because the council kept it for us, you and me. They built it from nothing and made it into a place where everyone can live peaceful-like, and do anything, say anything, be anyone. They kept it safe and protected it from… well… (Pause.) Can't you see? The council takes care of things.

(WEBER crosses back and sits downstage left.)

ASH

Are you sure?

(A plump, finely dressed RICH MAN enters stage right and crosses toward ASH.)

RICH MAN

Well, here we are, yes? Pleasant day, no?

(ASH and WEBER both turn to look at the man. They remain motionless.)

RICH MAN

Well speak up men. Time waits for no one, you know?

ASH

Hi.

WEBER

Hello.

ASH

Hello.

RICH MAN

Well, that's better, good. I'm a firm believer in… uh… in… in you, yes.

(WEBER rises and crosses to center.)

WEBER

I am Weber.

                    ASH
I'm Ash.

                    RICH MAN
Ah, good to meet you, both of you. I hear
good things about you, yes I do.

                    (WEBER and ASH look at
                    each other confusedly.)

                    RICH MAN (CONT)
Well good then.

                    WEBER
Excuse me, but who are—

                    RICH MAN
Oh yes, me, of course. I am one of the many,
but one of the few who helps choose members
for the council of civil improvement, yes. I
support the council financially with
monetary assets beyond the requested tribute
amounts and influentially through the
numerous public liaisons acquired in a long
and fruitful career.

                    (Pause. ASH turns and
                    looks blankly at WEBER.)

                    RICH MAN (CONT)
Basically what I'm here for is to broaden
the opportunities for people, such as
yourselves, in this great land of ours, so
that the good work the council does can
continue in a healthy and… uh… profitable
state.

(Pause. WEBER and ASH look confusedly at each other.

WEBER & ASH
(Together.) Of course.

RICH MAN
What I'm saying, quite simply, is that I am willing to support the best person seeking to be chosen for council, and I am told that it is one of you two.

WEBER
Council, oh yes, hello sir. (Extending his hand.) I am Weber.

ASH
(Extending his hand quickly.) I am Ash.

RICH MAN
Yes, yes you are, aren't you. Well, needless to say, only one of you can be the, how should I say, more agreeable person for the council.

WEBER
Agreeable?

RICH MAN
Yes.

WEBER
Of course, I see, what can I do for you—soup, or a slice of white bread?

ASH
No, how 'bout a nice bicycle—red if you like?

RICH MAN
No, no, I really have everything I could ever desire. My only wish is for my dear poodle, Dellie. She has, poor dear, a bad kidney on her left side, and needs to have a change soon or the pain of daily function may end her sweet life.

ASH
A dog?

RICH MAN
Dellie, my fine sir, is as human as any of the ramblers that roam about aimlessly, with no drive or motivation. A dog, perhaps, but a fine contributor to the intricate pattern of life in this land no doubt as well.

WEBER
Dellie needs a kidney?

RICH MAN
If you want my support, yes.

ASH
This is awkward. Kidneys and legs and dear dogs—

WEBER
(Excitedly.) Legs, of course. Sir, I will have a kidney for Dellie if I am chosen for the council.

RICH MAN
Will you, indeed?

                    WEBER
I know a man who could easily spare a kidney
for you. He's missing two legs already. One
kidney less would hardly be noticed.

                    ASH
You would take his kidney, too?

                    WEBER
(To the RICH MAN.) Good sir, believe me, the
man would not miss a kidney with his legs
gone before.

                    ASH
Then the kidney is mine.

                    WEBER
What?

                    ASH
He supports me for the council.

                    WEBER
No.

                    ASH
(To RICH MAN.) I will bring you a kidney for
your dear Dellie.

                    WEBER
Not from my beggar. His choice was for me.

                    ASH
His choice is for me now, and his kidney
with it.

                    WEBER
A thumbnail is yours.

ASH
You can keep the thumbnail, his whole hand if you want, but the kidney is mine. I have my rights, you know?

RICH MAN
Ah, such driving ambition will sustain the world. Time led by a heated hand follows the way of history before it.

(ASH looks at his hands.)

WEBER
Heated hand?

RICH MAN
Yes, of course heat. The blood of a councilor runs fierce. His heart and his mind, machines of a system, machines of method. Machines indeed, you say. Yes. Machines beyond insight, machines beyond truth. The breed of a councilor must rise above truth. Ideals and virtue are for the weak in spirit. One must rise to the trials of out day—trials of appearance, trials of rhetoric. The substance beneath is of little importance. Profit must guide the logic of man, and goal without profit is flawed in concept.

(UNA enters upstage left. The RICH MAN who has paced to downstage right in the course of his line is unaware of her presence.)

RICH MAN
(To WEBER.) Why give out soup, no one gave it to you?

                    UNA
Then your purpose becomes shallow, your
system hollow.

                         (The RICH MAN turns,
                         seemingly startled by UNA.
                         WEBER and ASH turn as
                         well.)

                    RICH MAN
Uh… well… not hollow—efficient. The council
survives as it always has, because it is
what works best.

                    WEBER
And when I'm on the council, I will do what
works best.

                    RICH MAN
(Smugly.) Yes, of course you will.

                    UNA
Don't you see? What he says works best will
keep everything the same. The good you can
do will be shut up and tied down—choked and
killed.

                    WEBER & ASH
(Together.) What do you mean?

                    RICH MAN
She means to keep you from what is
rightfully yours. On the council you could
have whatever you want, do whatever you
like. Don't be concerned so much about
change. The best cannot change the method of
ages past. And who is she to teach you
change?

ASH

Who is she?

WEBER

Who? I don't know.

ASH

Don't know her.

WEBER

Don't know.

RICH MAN

(He laughs.) No one is made to redirect human nature. Close your eyes and imagine a paradise.

(WEBER and ASH turn and look out over the audience, away from UNA. They close their eyes. The RICH MAN smiles and turns to UNA.)

RICH MAN

(To UNA.) Nothing can change when the interest lies elsewhere. In the depth of our hearts, we are all indifferent, and history will repeat.

(The RICH MAN exits downstage right.)

UNA

Yes, until they see the way. (Pause.)

ASH

Clam chowder.

                        WEBER
Beef and potato.

                        UNA
A duel to the death.

                        (UNA removes a case
                        containing two dueling
                        pistols from her jacket.
                        WEBER and ASH, take one
                        each, raise it to their
                        chest, and turn their
                        backs to each other.)

                        UNA
Won't you stay awake?

                        WEBER
It's ten thirty-seven.

                        UNA
Then it must be done.

                        (UNA exits upstage right.
                        WEBER and ASH begin their
                        paces away from each
                        other. WEBER exits stage
                        right. ASH exits stage
                        left. The lights slowly
                        change from the evening
                        blue to an unnatural,
                        blood red. After a long
                        period of silence, a
                        single deafening gunshot
                        is heard echoing through a
                        speaker backstage. The
                        lights slowly change back

to the moonlight of before. WEBER enters stage right as ASH enters stage left. Neither has a pistol. They stand downstage and stare out over the audience.)

                    WEBER
Dead?

                    ASH
I think so.

                    WEBER
Too dark to tell.

                    ASH
Too dark to see.

                    WEBER
Dead.

                    ASH
Can you see now?

                    WEBER
I think so. The moon is bright.

                    ASH
I thought it was you first, then the beggar.

                    WEBER
Too hard to tell.

                    ASH
Too hard to see.

                    WEBER
It wasn't the beggar.

ASH
No, I don't think so.

WEBER
Did you shoot too?

ASH
I suppose so.

WEBER
I couldn't tell.

ASH
I didn't see.

WEBER
It was her.

ASH
Yes, it was.

(Suddenly the VOICE filters in through the speaker again.)

VOICE
Hello, how are you?

WEBER
I'm fine. How are you?

VOICE
Just fine, thanks. I was just wondering... do you know what time it is?

WEBER
Does it really matter?

VOICE
Perhaps it could.

WEBER
She's dead you know.

VOICE
I know.

WEBER
It's been so dark.

VOICE
Morning will come.

WEBER
I suppose so.

VOICE
Don't worry too much Weber. The scene was plotted in my outline. All you did was fill in the gaps. If everyone could see what I've tried to work out, the time spent here could very well matter.

WEBER
But I didn't change a thing.

VOICE
Not yet. You are like many, many like yourself. But don't worry. You are all just characters in a mindful drama—images of an overly concerned imagination perhaps. Reality would never stand for such a treatment. Go home Weber. You can't sleep on this stage anymore.

(WEBER rises. He crosses to ASH and looks down at him, still staring over the audience. WEBER exits stage left.)

(Lights fade out.)

Scene 8

(The next morning. The lights fade up to suggest morning. WEBER is digging what appears to be a grave, center stage near his rock. After a while, ASH enters stage right, carrying a small tree. He places it in the hole and they begin to plant it together.)

(Lights fade out.)

The End

about the playwright

Paolo Mazzucato is an author, playwright and screenwriter. He attended Northwestern University in Evanston, Illinois, and wrote POLITICOS when he was a student in their pilot Creative Writing for the Media Program. He submitted the finished play to a handful of Chicago theaters, and it was selected for production in the 1988 New Works and New Genres Series at the Organic Theater Company.

www.ingramcontent.com/pod-product-compliance
Lightning Source LLC
Chambersburg PA
CBHW021122080526
44587CB00010B/610